PRAY WITH A PEN

A 13-WEEK JOURNAL
FOR PRAYING & PLANNING

JUSTIN HYDE

LUCIDBOOKS

Pray with a Pen
A 13-Week Journal for Praying and Planning

Copyright © 2018 by Justin Hyde

Published by Lucid Books in Houston, TX
www.LucidBooksPublishing.com

ISBN-10: 1-63296-305-1
ISBN-13: 978-1-63296-305-5

Introduction

I'm distracted when I pray.

When I sit down to pray, my thoughts often splinter into unrelated fragments. My mind goes to a sin I need to confess. To gratitude for my children. To the overwhelming needs of my friends, family, and church members. To my to-do lists. To my savings account. To a health worry. To the movie my wife and I watched last night. To . . . and I'm already off track.

I struggle to regain focus, and as a result, my times of prayer are sometimes anemic and impersonal. Distraction reduces affection. Through listening and responding to God in prayer, I hope to increase my knowledge and love of scripture, to expose my soul to God for conviction and refreshment, to cultivate a relationship with the Persons of God (to enjoy, in the words of John Calvin, "an intimate conversation"), and, among other things, to be obedient.

What I found most helpful was to *pray with a pen*. Praying with a pen gives me a written record of God's faithfulness. I am humbled (and made more grateful) as I review the pages of previous days and decades. Praying with a pen also helps me pray within a structure that I have enjoyed for years: Adoration, Confession, Thanksgiving, and Supplication.

This A.C.T.S. method, the same method I used to teach my children to pray, somehow both anchors me within myself (I am more aware of my sin) and lifts my attention toward God (I am more aware of his beauty, complexity, and goodness).

Through focused Adoration, I reflect on the God-ness of God. "Lord, you are creative. You are consistent. You are always present. You are good to your creation. You give freely. You are wholly trustworthy."

Through focused Confession, I consider my sins—both specific and general—and in the act of writing, I experience the sting of my rebellion and the intensity of God's forgiveness.

Through focused Thanksgiving, I push through a vague sense of appreciation to a more profound awareness of God's detailed favor.

Through focused Supplication, I rein in the paralyzing effect of considering innumerable needs and can simply "let my requests be made known to God" (Phil. 4:6), which—as promised—reduces my anxiety.

Of course, a person can pray without a pen . . . and in fact we all should "pray without ceasing" (1 Thess. 5:17) through the minutia of our rhythms and relationships. But the discipline of writing has its benefits.

In addition to structured prayer, I have added contemplative questions to consider each quarter, each week, and each day as well as space to consider your most pressing goals. I include these here, because I want to eliminate the chasm between our prayers and our plans. One must shape the other. Considering these questions on a regular basis has been a help to this particularly distracted person. I hope they are helpful for you.

Pray and plan—with pen in hand—and "may [God] grant you your heart's desire and fulfill all your plans" (Psalm 20:4)!

Justin Hyde

How to Use this Journal

This journal is organized around a 13-week schedule.

At the beginning of the journal, there is a place to outline your quarterly prayer concerns, plans, and goals. These are big picture and long term. At the beginning of each week, there is a place to outline more immediate prayers and goals. As mentioned in the introduction, there is nothing magical about these questions or this methodology, but these have been particularly helpful to review on a regular basis. Goal-setting is broken into three elements: your Goal (*What* do I want?); your Motivation (*Why* do I want it?); and your Action (*How* will I get it?).

There is space each day to meditate on scripture, record prayer concerns, set goals, and make notes. You can use Adoration, Confession, Thanksgiving, and Supplication (A.C.T.S.) to organize your prayers, but don't feel limited by that method.

After every four weeks, the journal includes 20 questions for self-reflection.

13 WEEKS OF PRAYERS
AND PLANS

Today's Date:_____

What am I praying for this quarter?

_____

_____

_____

_____

What I am thankful for from last quarter?

_____

_____

_____

_____

What am I excited about this quarter?

_____

_____

_____

_____

What are my biggest challenges this quarter?

_____

_____

_____

_____

How can I make the deepest impact this quarter?

_____

_____

_____

_____

_____

_____

_____

Top Three Goals This Quarter:

What's the most important objective I plan to accomplish this quarter?
Goal (What do I want?):

_____

Motivation (Why do I want it?):

_____

Action (How will I get it?):

_____

What's the second-most important objective I plan to accomplish this quarter?
Goal (What do I want?):

_____

Motivation (Why do I want it?):

_____

Action (How will I get it?):

_____

What's the third-most important objective I plan to accomplish this quarter?
Goal (What do I want?):

_____

Motivation (Why do I want it?):

_____

Action (How will I get it?):

_____

WEEK 1

Today's Date: _____

What am I praying for this week?

_____

_____

_____

What I am thankful for from last week?

_____

_____

_____

What am I excited about this week?

_____

_____

_____

What are my biggest challenges this week?

_____

_____

_____

How can I make the deepest impact this week?

_____

_____

_____

Top Three Goals This Week:

Goal #1

Goal (What do I want?):

_____

Motivation (Why do I want it?):

_____

Action (How will I get it?):

_____

Goal #2

Goal (What do I want?):

_____

Motivation (Why do I want it?):

_____

Action (How will I get it?):

_____

Goal #3

Goal (What do I want?):

_____

Motivation (Why do I want it?):

_____

Action (How will I get it?):

_____

WEEK 1
DAY 1

Today's Date:_____

Scripture to Consider:_____

Reflections on Scripture:_____

_____

Adoration:_____

_____

_____

Confession:_____

_____

_____

Thanksgiving:_____

_____

_____

Supplication:_____

_____

_____

What's the most important thing I plan to do today?

_____

_____

Whom can I serve (encourage, bless, invest in, etc.) today?

_____

_____

How?

_____

_____

How am I doing on my weekly goals?

_____

_____

Notes:

_____

_____

_____

_____

_____

_____

_____

_____

_____

_____

Today's Date:_____

Scripture to Consider:_____

Reflections on Scripture:_____

_____

Adoration:_____

_____

_____

Confession:_____

_____

_____

Thanksgiving:_____

_____

_____

Supplication:_____

_____

_____

What's the most important thing I plan to do today?

_____

_____

Whom can I serve (encourage, bless, invest in, etc.) today?

_____

_____

How?

_____

_____

How am I doing on my weekly goals?

_____

_____

Notes:

_____

_____

_____

_____

_____

_____

_____

_____

_____

_____

Today's Date:_____

Scripture to Consider:_____

Reflections on Scripture:_____

_____

Adoration:_____

_____

_____

Confession:_____

_____

_____

Thanksgiving:_____

_____

_____

Supplication:_____

_____

_____

What's the most important thing I plan to do today?

_____

_____

Whom can I serve (encourage, bless, invest in, etc.) today?

_____

_____

How?

_____

_____

How am I doing on my weekly goals?

_____

_____

Notes:

_____

_____

_____

_____

_____

_____

_____

_____

_____

_____

_____

Today's Date:_____

Scripture to Consider:_____

Reflections on Scripture:_____

_____

Adoration:_____

_____

_____

Confession:_____

_____

_____

Thanksgiving:_____

_____

_____

Supplication:_____

_____

_____

What's the most important thing I plan to do today?

_____

_____

Whom can I serve (encourage, bless, invest in, etc.) today?

_____

_____

How?

_____

_____

How am I doing on my weekly goals?

_____

_____

Notes:

_____

_____

_____

_____

_____

_____

_____

_____

_____

_____

Today's Date:_____

Scripture to Consider:_____

Reflections on Scripture:_____

_____

Adoration:_____

_____

_____

Confession:_____

_____

_____

Thanksgiving:_____

_____

_____

Supplication:_____

_____

_____

What's the most important thing I plan to do today?

_____

_____

Whom can I serve (encourage, bless, invest in, etc.) today?

_____

_____

How?

_____

_____

How am I doing on my weekly goals?

_____

_____

Notes:

_____

_____

_____

_____

_____

_____

_____

_____

_____

_____

_____

WEEK 1
DAY 6

Today's Date:_____

Scripture to Consider: _____

Reflections on Scripture:_____
_____

Adoration:_____
_____
_____

Confession:_____
_____
_____

Thanksgiving:_____
_____
_____

Supplication:_____
_____
_____

What's the most important thing I plan to do today?

_____

_____

Whom can I serve (encourage, bless, invest in, etc.) today?

_____

_____

How?

_____

_____

How am I doing on my weekly goals?

_____

_____

Notes:

_____

_____

_____

_____

_____

_____

_____

_____

_____

_____

Today's Date:_____

Scripture to Consider:_____

Reflections on Scripture:_____

_____

Adoration:_____

_____

_____

Confession:_____

_____

_____

Thanksgiving:_____

_____

_____

Supplication:_____

_____

_____

What's the most important thing I plan to do today?

_____

_____

Whom can I serve (encourage, bless, invest in, etc.) today?

_____

_____

How?

_____

_____

How am I doing on my weekly goals?

_____

_____

Notes:

_____

_____

_____

_____

_____

_____

_____

_____

_____

_____

WEEK 2

Today's Date:_____

What am I praying for this week?

_____

_____

_____

What I am thankful for from last week?

_____

_____

_____

What am I excited about this week?

_____

_____

_____

What are my biggest challenges this week?

_____

_____

_____

How can I make the deepest impact this week?

_____

_____

_____

Top Three Goals This Week:

Goal #1

Goal (What do I want?):

_____

Motivation (Why do I want it?):

_____

Action (How will I get it?):

_____

Goal #2

Goal (What do I want?):

_____

Motivation (Why do I want it?):

_____

Action (How will I get it?):

_____

Goal #3

Goal (What do I want?):

_____

Motivation (Why do I want it?):

_____

Action (How will I get it?):

_____

Today's Date:_____

Scripture to Consider:_____

Reflections on Scripture:_____

_____

Adoration:_____

_____

_____

Confession:_____

_____

_____

Thanksgiving:_____

_____

_____

Supplication:_____

_____

_____

What's the most important thing I plan to do today?

_____

_____

Whom can I serve (encourage, bless, invest in, etc.) today?

_____

_____

How?

_____

_____

How am I doing on my weekly goals?

_____

_____

Notes:

_____

_____

_____

_____

_____

_____

_____

_____

_____

_____

WEEK 2
DAY 2

Today's Date:_____

Scripture to Consider: _____

Reflections on Scripture:_____

_____

Adoration: _____

_____

_____

Confession:_____

_____

_____

Thanksgiving:_____

_____

_____

Supplication: _____

_____

_____

What's the most important thing I plan to do today?

_____

_____

Whom can I serve (encourage, bless, invest in, etc.) today?

_____

_____

How?

_____

_____

How am I doing on my weekly goals?

_____

_____

Notes:

_____

_____

_____

_____

_____

_____

_____

_____

_____

_____

WEEK 2
DAY 3

Today's Date:_____

Scripture to Consider:_____

Reflections on Scripture:_____

_____

Adoration:_____

_____

_____

Confession:_____

_____

_____

Thanksgiving:_____

_____

_____

Supplication:_____

_____

_____

What's the most important thing I plan to do today?

_____

_____

Whom can I serve (encourage, bless, invest in, etc.) today?

_____

_____

How?

_____

_____

How am I doing on my weekly goals?

_____

_____

Notes:

_____

_____

_____

_____

_____

_____

_____

_____

_____

_____

_____

Today's Date:_____

Scripture to Consider:_____

Reflections on Scripture:_____

_____

Adoration:_____

_____

_____

Confession:_____

_____

_____

Thanksgiving:_____

_____

_____

Supplication:_____

_____

_____

What's the most important thing I plan to do today?

_____

_____

Whom can I serve (encourage, bless, invest in, etc.) today?

_____

_____

How?

_____

_____

How am I doing on my weekly goals?

_____

_____

Notes:

_____

_____

_____

_____

_____

_____

_____

_____

_____

_____

Today's Date:_____

Scripture to Consider: _____

Reflections on Scripture:_____

_____

Adoration: _____

_____

_____

Confession: _____

_____

_____

Thanksgiving:_____

_____

_____

Supplication: _____

_____

_____

What's the most important thing I plan to do today?

_____

_____

Whom can I serve (encourage, bless, invest in, etc.) today?

_____

_____

How?

_____

_____

How am I doing on my weekly goals?

_____

_____

Notes:

_____

_____

_____

_____

_____

_____

_____

_____

_____

_____

WEEK 2
DAY 6

Today's Date:_____

Scripture to Consider:_____

Reflections on Scripture:_____

_____

Adoration:_____

_____

_____

Confession:_____

_____

_____

Thanksgiving:_____

_____

_____

Supplication:_____

_____

_____

What's the most important thing I plan to do today?

_____

_____

Whom can I serve (encourage, bless, invest in, etc.) today?

_____

_____

How?

_____

_____

How am I doing on my weekly goals?

_____

_____

Notes:

_____

_____

_____

_____

_____

_____

_____

_____

_____

_____

WEEK 2
DAY 7

Today's Date: _____

Scripture to Consider: _____

Reflections on Scripture: _____

_____

Adoration: _____

_____

_____

Confession: _____

_____

_____

Thanksgiving: _____

_____

_____

Supplication: _____

_____

_____

What's the most important thing I plan to do today?

_____

_____

Whom can I serve (encourage, bless, invest in, etc.) today?

_____

_____

How?

_____

_____

How am I doing on my weekly goals?

_____

_____

Notes:

_____

_____

_____

_____

_____

_____

_____

_____

_____

_____

WEEK 3

Today's Date:_____

What am I praying for this week?

_____

_____

_____

What I am thankful for from last week?

_____

_____

_____

What am I excited about this week?

_____

_____

_____

What are my biggest challenges this week?

_____

_____

_____

How can I make the deepest impact this week?

_____

_____

_____

Top Three Goals This Week:

Goal #1

Goal (What do I want?):

_____

Motivation (Why do I want it?):

_____

Action (How will I get it?):

_____

Goal #2

Goal (What do I want?):

_____

Motivation (Why do I want it?):

_____

Action (How will I get it?):

_____

Goal #3

Goal (What do I want?):

_____

Motivation (Why do I want it?):

_____

Action (How will I get it?):

_____

WEEK 3
DAY 1

Today's Date:_____

Scripture to Consider:_____

Reflections on Scripture:_____

_____

Adoration:_____

_____

_____

Confession:_____

_____

_____

Thanksgiving:_____

_____

_____

Supplication:_____

_____

_____

What's the most important thing I plan to do today?

_____

_____

Whom can I serve (encourage, bless, invest in, etc.) today?

_____

_____

How?

_____

_____

How am I doing on my weekly goals?

_____

_____

Notes:

_____

_____

_____

_____

_____

_____

_____

_____

_____

_____

WEEK 3
DAY 2

Today's Date:_____

Scripture to Consider:_____

Reflections on Scripture:_____

_____

Adoration:_____

_____

_____

Confession:_____

_____

_____

Thanksgiving:_____

_____

_____

Supplication:_____

_____

_____

What's the most important thing I plan to do today?

_____

_____

Whom can I serve (encourage, bless, invest in, etc.) today?

_____

_____

How?

_____

_____

How am I doing on my weekly goals?

_____

_____

Notes:

_____

_____

_____

_____

_____

_____

_____

_____

_____

_____

Today's Date:_____

Scripture to Consider:_____

Reflections on Scripture:_____

_____

Adoration:_____

_____

_____

Confession:_____

_____

_____

Thanksgiving:_____

_____

_____

Supplication:_____

_____

_____

What's the most important thing I plan to do today?

_____

_____

Whom can I serve (encourage, bless, invest in, etc.) today?

_____

_____

How?

_____

_____

How am I doing on my weekly goals?

_____

_____

Notes:

_____

_____

_____

_____

_____

_____

_____

_____

_____

WEEK 3
DAY 4

Today's Date:_____

Scripture to Consider:_____

Reflections on Scripture:_____

_____

Adoration:_____

_____

_____

Confession:_____

_____

_____

Thanksgiving:_____

_____

_____

Supplication:_____

_____

_____

What's the most important thing I plan to do today?

_____

_____

Whom can I serve (encourage, bless, invest in, etc.) today?

_____

_____

How?

_____

_____

How am I doing on my weekly goals?

_____

_____

Notes:

_____

_____

_____

_____

_____

_____

_____

_____

_____

_____

Today's Date: _____

Scripture to Consider: _____

Reflections on Scripture: _____

_____

Adoration: _____

_____

_____

Confession: _____

_____

_____

Thanksgiving: _____

_____

_____

Supplication: _____

_____

_____

What's the most important thing I plan to do today?

_____

_____

Whom can I serve (encourage, bless, invest in, etc.) today?

_____

_____

How?

_____

_____

How am I doing on my weekly goals?

_____

_____

Notes:

_____

_____

_____

_____

_____

_____

_____

_____

_____

_____

_____

WEEK 3
DAY 6

Today's Date:_____

Scripture to Consider:_____

Reflections on Scripture:_____

_____

Adoration:_____

_____

_____

Confession:_____

_____

_____

Thanksgiving:_____

_____

_____

Supplication:_____

_____

_____

What's the most important thing I plan to do today?

_____

_____

Whom can I serve (encourage, bless, invest in, etc.) today?

_____

_____

How?

_____

_____

How am I doing on my weekly goals?

_____

_____

Notes:

_____

_____

_____

_____

_____

_____

_____

_____

_____

_____

Today's Date:_____

Scripture to Consider: _____

Reflections on Scripture:_____

_____

Adoration: _____

_____

_____

Confession: _____

_____

_____

Thanksgiving:_____

_____

_____

Supplication: _____

_____

_____

What's the most important thing I plan to do today?

_____

_____

Whom can I serve (encourage, bless, invest in, etc.) today?

_____

_____

How?

_____

_____

How am I doing on my weekly goals?

_____

_____

Notes:

_____

_____

_____

_____

_____

_____

_____

_____

_____

_____

WEEK 4

Today's Date:_____

What am I praying for this week?

_____

_____

_____

What I am thankful for from last week?

_____

_____

_____

What am I excited about this week?

_____

_____

_____

What are my biggest challenges this week?

_____

_____

_____

How can I make the deepest impact this week?

_____

_____

_____

Top Three Goals This Week:

Goal #1

Goal (What do I want?):

_____

Motivation (Why do I want it?):

_____

Action (How will I get it?):

_____

Goal #2

Goal (What do I want?):

_____

Motivation (Why do I want it?):

_____

Action (How will I get it?):

_____

Goal #3

Goal (What do I want?):

_____

Motivation (Why do I want it?):

_____

Action (How will I get it?):

_____

WEEK 4
DAY 1

Today's Date:_____

Scripture to Consider:_____

Reflections on Scripture:_____

_____

Adoration:_____

_____

_____

Confession:_____

_____

_____

Thanksgiving:_____

_____

_____

Supplication:_____

_____

_____

What's the most important thing I plan to do today?

_____

_____

Whom can I serve (encourage, bless, invest in, etc.) today?

_____

_____

How?

_____

_____

How am I doing on my weekly goals?

_____

_____

Notes:

_____

_____

_____

_____

_____

_____

_____

_____

_____

_____

WEEK 4
DAY 2

Today's Date:_____

Scripture to Consider: _____

Reflections on Scripture:_____

_____

Adoration: _____

_____

_____

Confession:_____

_____

_____

Thanksgiving:_____

_____

_____

Supplication:_____

_____

_____

What's the most important thing I plan to do today?

_____

_____

Whom can I serve (encourage, bless, invest in, etc.) today?

_____

_____

How?

_____

_____

How am I doing on my weekly goals?

_____

_____

Notes:

_____

_____

_____

_____

_____

_____

_____

_____

_____

_____

Today's Date: _____

Scripture to Consider: _____

Reflections on Scripture: _____

_____

Adoration: _____

_____

_____

Confession: _____

_____

_____

Thanksgiving: _____

_____

_____

Supplication: _____

_____

_____

What's the most important thing I plan to do today?

_____

_____

Whom can I serve (encourage, bless, invest in, etc.) today?

_____

_____

How?

_____

_____

How am I doing on my weekly goals?

_____

_____

Notes:

_____

_____

_____

_____

_____

_____

_____

_____

_____

_____

Today's Date:_____

Scripture to Consider:_____

Reflections on Scripture:_____

_____

Adoration:_____

_____

_____

Confession:_____

_____

_____

Thanksgiving:_____

_____

_____

Supplication:_____

_____

_____

What's the most important thing I plan to do today?

_____

_____

Whom can I serve (encourage, bless, invest in, etc.) today?

_____

_____

How?

_____

_____

How am I doing on my weekly goals?

_____

_____

Notes:

_____

_____

_____

_____

_____

_____

_____

_____

_____

_____

WEEK 4
DAY 5

Today's Date:_____

Scripture to Consider:_____

Reflections on Scripture:_____

_____

Adoration:_____

_____

_____

Confession:_____

_____

_____

Thanksgiving:_____

_____

_____

Supplication:_____

_____

_____

What's the most important thing I plan to do today?

_____

_____

Whom can I serve (encourage, bless, invest in, etc.) today?

_____

_____

How?

_____

_____

How am I doing on my weekly goals?

_____

_____

Notes:

_____

_____

_____

_____

_____

_____

_____

_____

_____

_____

Today's Date:_____

Scripture to Consider:_____

Reflections on Scripture:_____

_____

Adoration:_____

_____

_____

Confession:_____

_____

_____

Thanksgiving:_____

_____

_____

Supplication:_____

_____

_____

What's the most important thing I plan to do today?

_____

_____

Whom can I serve (encourage, bless, invest in, etc.) today?

_____

_____

How?

_____

_____

How am I doing on my weekly goals?

_____

_____

Notes:

_____

_____

_____

_____

_____

_____

_____

_____

_____

_____

_____

Today's Date:_____

Scripture to Consider:_____

Reflections on Scripture:_____

_____

Adoration:_____

_____

_____

Confession:_____

_____

_____

Thanksgiving:_____

_____

_____

Supplication:_____

_____

_____

What's the most important thing I plan to do today?

_____

_____

Whom can I serve (encourage, bless, invest in, etc.) today?

_____

_____

How?

_____

_____

How am I doing on my weekly goals?

_____

_____

Notes:

_____

_____

_____

_____

_____

_____

_____

_____

_____

_____

20 MONTHLY QUESTIONS
FOR SELF-REFLECTION

What has God accomplished in my character in the last four weeks?

_____

_____

_____

How has God shown his faithfulness to me in the last four weeks?

_____

_____

_____

What passage of scripture has had the most impact over the last four weeks?

_____

_____

_____

What was my last powerful experience with God?

_____

_____

_____

What is increasing my affection toward God and others?

_____

_____

_____

What is decreasing my affection toward God and others?

_____

_____

_____

What is causing me fear or anxiety right now?

_____

_____

_____

Where is my heart hard or cold?

_____

_____

_____

What do I need most from God right now?

_____

_____

_____

Where am I most encouraged?

_____

_____

_____

Where am I most discouraged?

_____

_____

_____

What areas of my life most need to be transformed?

_____

_____

_____

What current obstacles hinder my spiritual growth?

_____

_____

_____

What competes with God for my affection and attention?

_____

_____

_____

What bad habits do I need to avoid?

_____

_____

_____

What good habits do I need to grow?

_____

_____

_____

Which relationships need to improve? How?

_____

_____

_____

What am I taking for granted?

_____

_____

_____

How am I doing with my quarterly goals?

_____

_____

_____

What actions do I need to take based on these questions?

_____

_____

_____

WEEK 5

Today's Date:_____

What am I praying for this week?

_____

_____

_____

What I am thankful for from last week?

_____

_____

_____

What am I excited about this week?

_____

_____

_____

What are my biggest challenges this week?

_____

_____

_____

How can I make the deepest impact this week?

_____

_____

_____

Top Three Goals This Week:

Goal #1

Goal (What do I want?):

_____

Motivation (Why do I want it?):

_____

Action (How will I get it?):

_____

Goal #2

Goal (What do I want?):

_____

Motivation (Why do I want it?):

_____

Action (How will I get it?):

_____

Goal #3

Goal (What do I want?):

_____

Motivation (Why do I want it?):

_____

Action (How will I get it?):

_____

WEEK 5
DAY 1

Today's Date:_____

Scripture to Consider: _____

Reflections on Scripture:_____

_____

Adoration: _____

_____

_____

Confession:_____

_____

_____

Thanksgiving:_____

_____

_____

Supplication: _____

_____

_____

What's the most important thing I plan to do today?

_____

_____

Whom can I serve (encourage, bless, invest in, etc.) today?

_____

_____

How?

_____

_____

How am I doing on my weekly goals?

_____

_____

Notes:

_____

_____

_____

_____

_____

_____

_____

_____

_____

_____

_____

Today's Date: _____

Scripture to Consider: _____

Reflections on Scripture: _____

_____

Adoration: _____

_____

_____

Confession: _____

_____

_____

Thanksgiving: _____

_____

_____

Supplication: _____

_____

_____

What's the most important thing I plan to do today?

_____

_____

Whom can I serve (encourage, bless, invest in, etc.) today?

_____

_____

How?

_____

_____

How am I doing on my weekly goals?

_____

_____

Notes:

_____

_____

_____

_____

_____

_____

_____

_____

_____

_____

_____

Today's Date:_____

Scripture to Consider:_____

Reflections on Scripture:_____

_____

Adoration:_____

_____

_____

Confession:_____

_____

_____

Thanksgiving:_____

_____

_____

Supplication:_____

_____

_____

What's the most important thing I plan to do today?

_____

_____

Whom can I serve (encourage, bless, invest in, etc.) today?

_____

_____

How?

_____

_____

How am I doing on my weekly goals?

_____

_____

Notes:

_____

_____

_____

_____

_____

_____

_____

_____

_____

_____

WEEK 5
DAY 4

Today's Date:_____

Scripture to Consider:_____

Reflections on Scripture:_____

_____

Adoration:_____

_____

_____

Confession:_____

_____

_____

Thanksgiving:_____

_____

_____

Supplication:_____

_____

_____

What's the most important thing I plan to do today?

_____

_____

Whom can I serve (encourage, bless, invest in, etc.) today?

_____

_____

How?

_____

_____

How am I doing on my weekly goals?

_____

_____

Notes:

_____

_____

_____

_____

_____

_____

_____

_____

_____

_____

WEEK 5
DAY 5

Today's Date:_____

Scripture to Consider:_____

Reflections on Scripture:_____

_____

Adoration:_____

_____

_____

Confession:_____

_____

_____

Thanksgiving:_____

_____

_____

Supplication:_____

_____

_____

What's the most important thing I plan to do today?

_____

_____

Whom can I serve (encourage, bless, invest in, etc.) today?

_____

_____

How?

_____

_____

How am I doing on my weekly goals?

_____

_____

Notes:

_____

_____

_____

_____

_____

_____

_____

_____

_____

_____

Today's Date:_____

Scripture to Consider:_____

Reflections on Scripture:_____

_____

Adoration:_____

_____

_____

Confession:_____

_____

_____

Thanksgiving:_____

_____

_____

Supplication:_____

_____

_____

What's the most important thing I plan to do today?

_____

_____

Whom can I serve (encourage, bless, invest in, etc.) today?

_____

_____

How?

_____

_____

How am I doing on my weekly goals?

_____

_____

Notes:

_____

_____

_____

_____

_____

_____

_____

_____

_____

_____

Today's Date:_____

Scripture to Consider:_____

Reflections on Scripture:_____

_____

Adoration:_____

_____

_____

Confession:_____

_____

_____

Thanksgiving:_____

_____

_____

Supplication:_____

_____

_____

What's the most important thing I plan to do today?

_____

_____

Whom can I serve (encourage, bless, invest in, etc.) today?

_____

_____

How?

_____

_____

How am I doing on my weekly goals?

_____

_____

Notes:

_____

_____

_____

_____

_____

_____

_____

_____

_____

_____

WEEK 6

Today's Date:_____

What am I praying for this week?

_____

_____

_____

What I am thankful for from last week?

_____

_____

_____

What am I excited about this week?

_____

_____

_____

What are my biggest challenges this week?

_____

_____

_____

How can I make the deepest impact this week?

_____

_____

_____

Top Three Goals This Week:

Goal #1

Goal (What do I want?):

_____

Motivation (Why do I want it?):

_____

Action (How will I get it?):

_____

Goal #2

Goal (What do I want?):

_____

Motivation (Why do I want it?):

_____

Action (How will I get it?):

_____

Goal #3

Goal (What do I want?):

_____

Motivation (Why do I want it?):

_____

Action (How will I get it?):

_____

WEEK 6
DAY 1

Today's Date:_____

Scripture to Consider:_____

Reflections on Scripture:_____

_____

Adoration:_____

_____

_____

Confession:_____

_____

_____

Thanksgiving:_____

_____

_____

Supplication:_____

_____

_____

What's the most important thing I plan to do today?

_____

_____

Whom can I serve (encourage, bless, invest in, etc.) today?

_____

_____

How?

_____

_____

How am I doing on my weekly goals?

_____

_____

Notes:

_____

_____

_____

_____

_____

_____

_____

_____

_____

_____

Today's Date:_____

Scripture to Consider:_____

Reflections on Scripture:_____

_____

Adoration:_____

_____

_____

Confession:_____

_____

_____

Thanksgiving:_____

_____

_____

Supplication:_____

_____

_____

What's the most important thing I plan to do today?

_____

_____

Whom can I serve (encourage, bless, invest in, etc.) today?

_____

_____

How?

_____

_____

How am I doing on my weekly goals?

_____

_____

Notes:

_____

_____

_____

_____

_____

_____

_____

_____

_____

_____

WEEK 6
DAY 3

Today's Date: _____

Scripture to Consider: _____

Reflections on Scripture: _____

_____

Adoration: _____

_____

_____

Confession: _____

_____

_____

Thanksgiving: _____

_____

_____

Supplication: _____

_____

_____

What's the most important thing I plan to do today?

_____

_____

Whom can I serve (encourage, bless, invest in, etc.) today?

_____

_____

How?

_____

_____

How am I doing on my weekly goals?

_____

_____

Notes:

_____

_____

_____

_____

_____

_____

_____

_____

_____

_____

Today's Date: _____

Scripture to Consider: _____

Reflections on Scripture: _____

_____

Adoration: _____

_____

_____

Confession: _____

_____

_____

Thanksgiving: _____

_____

_____

Supplication: _____

_____

_____

What's the most important thing I plan to do today?

_____

_____

Whom can I serve (encourage, bless, invest in, etc.) today?

_____

_____

How?

_____

_____

How am I doing on my weekly goals?

_____

_____

Notes:

_____

_____

_____

_____

_____

_____

_____

_____

_____

Today's Date:_____

Scripture to Consider:_____

Reflections on Scripture:_____

_____

Adoration:_____

_____

_____

Confession:_____

_____

_____

Thanksgiving:_____

_____

_____

Supplication:_____

_____

_____

What's the most important thing I plan to do today?

_____

_____

Whom can I serve (encourage, bless, invest in, etc.) today?

_____

_____

How?

_____

_____

How am I doing on my weekly goals?

_____

_____

Notes:

_____

_____

_____

_____

_____

_____

_____

_____

_____

_____

Today's Date:_____

Scripture to Consider: _____

Reflections on Scripture:_____

_____

Adoration:_____

_____

_____

Confession:_____

_____

_____

Thanksgiving:_____

_____

_____

Supplication:_____

_____

_____

What's the most important thing I plan to do today?

_____

_____

Whom can I serve (encourage, bless, invest in, etc.) today?

_____

_____

How?

_____

_____

How am I doing on my weekly goals?

_____

_____

Notes:

_____

_____

_____

_____

_____

_____

_____

_____

_____

_____

_____

Today's Date:_____

Scripture to Consider:_____

Reflections on Scripture:_____

_____

Adoration:_____

_____

_____

Confession:_____

_____

_____

Thanksgiving:_____

_____

_____

Supplication:_____

_____

_____

What's the most important thing I plan to do today?

_____

_____

Whom can I serve (encourage, bless, invest in, etc.) today?

_____

_____

How?

_____

_____

How am I doing on my weekly goals?

_____

_____

Notes:

_____

_____

_____

_____

_____

_____

_____

_____

_____

_____

WEEK 7

Today's Date:_____

What am I praying for this week?

_____

_____

_____

What I am thankful for from last week?

_____

_____

_____

What am I excited about this week?

_____

_____

_____

What are my biggest challenges this week?

_____

_____

_____

How can I make the deepest impact this week?

_____

_____

_____

Top Three Goals This Week:

Goal #1

Goal (What do I want?):

_____

Motivation (Why do I want it?):

_____

Action (How will I get it?):

_____

Goal #2

Goal (What do I want?):

_____

Motivation (Why do I want it?):

_____

Action (How will I get it?):

_____

Goal #3

Goal (What do I want?):

_____

Motivation (Why do I want it?):

_____

Action (How will I get it?):

_____

Today's Date:_____

Scripture to Consider:_____

Reflections on Scripture:_____

_____

Adoration:_____

_____

_____

Confession:_____

_____

_____

Thanksgiving:_____

_____

_____

Supplication:_____

_____

_____

What's the most important thing I plan to do today?

_____

_____

Whom can I serve (encourage, bless, invest in, etc.) today?

_____

_____

How?

_____

_____

How am I doing on my weekly goals?

_____

_____

Notes:

_____

_____

_____

_____

_____

_____

_____

_____

_____

_____

Today's Date:_____

Scripture to Consider: _____

Reflections on Scripture:_____

_____

Adoration:_____

_____

_____

Confession:_____

_____

_____

Thanksgiving:_____

_____

_____

Supplication:_____

_____

_____

What's the most important thing I plan to do today?

_____

_____

Whom can I serve (encourage, bless, invest in, etc.) today?

_____

_____

How?

_____

_____

How am I doing on my weekly goals?

_____

_____

Notes:

_____

_____

_____

_____

_____

_____

_____

_____

_____

_____

Today's Date:_____

Scripture to Consider: _____

Reflections on Scripture:_____

_____

Adoration: _____

_____

_____

Confession:_____

_____

_____

Thanksgiving:_____

_____

_____

Supplication: _____

_____

_____

What's the most important thing I plan to do today?

_____

_____

Whom can I serve (encourage, bless, invest in, etc.) today?

_____

_____

How?

_____

_____

How am I doing on my weekly goals?

_____

_____

Notes:

_____

_____

_____

_____

_____

_____

_____

_____

_____

_____

Today's Date:_____

Scripture to Consider:_____

Reflections on Scripture:_____

_____

Adoration:_____

_____

_____

Confession:_____

_____

_____

Thanksgiving:_____

_____

_____

Supplication:_____

_____

_____

What's the most important thing I plan to do today?

_____

_____

Whom can I serve (encourage, bless, invest in, etc.) today?

_____

_____

How?

_____

_____

How am I doing on my weekly goals?

_____

_____

Notes:

_____

_____

_____

_____

_____

_____

_____

_____

_____

_____

Today's Date: _____

Scripture to Consider: _____

Reflections on Scripture: _____

_____

Adoration: _____

_____

_____

Confession: _____

_____

_____

Thanksgiving: _____

_____

_____

Supplication: _____

_____

_____

What's the most important thing I plan to do today?

_____

_____

Whom can I serve (encourage, bless, invest in, etc.) today?

_____

_____

How?

_____

_____

How am I doing on my weekly goals?

_____

_____

Notes:

_____

_____

_____

_____

_____

_____

_____

_____

_____

_____

_____

Today's Date:_____

Scripture to Consider: _____

Reflections on Scripture:_____

_____

Adoration:_____

_____

_____

Confession:_____

_____

_____

Thanksgiving:_____

_____

_____

Supplication: _____

_____

_____

What's the most important thing I plan to do today?

_____

_____

Whom can I serve (encourage, bless, invest in, etc.) today?

_____

_____

How?

_____

_____

How am I doing on my weekly goals?

_____

_____

Notes:

_____

_____

_____

_____

_____

_____

_____

_____

_____

_____

WEEK 7
DAY 7

Today's Date:_____

Scripture to Consider:_____

Reflections on Scripture:_____

_____

Adoration:_____

_____

_____

Confession:_____

_____

_____

Thanksgiving:_____

_____

_____

Supplication:_____

_____

_____

What's the most important thing I plan to do today?

_____

_____

Whom can I serve (encourage, bless, invest in, etc.) today?

_____

_____

How?

_____

_____

How am I doing on my weekly goals?

_____

_____

Notes:

_____

_____

_____

_____

_____

_____

_____

_____

_____

_____

WEEK 8

Today's Date:_____

What am I praying for this week?

_____

_____

_____

What I am thankful for from last week?

_____

_____

_____

What am I excited about this week?

_____

_____

_____

What are my biggest challenges this week?

_____

_____

_____

How can I make the deepest impact this week?

_____

_____

_____

Top Three Goals This Week:

Goal #1

Goal (What do I want?):

_____

Motivation (Why do I want it?):

_____

Action (How will I get it?):

_____

Goal #2

Goal (What do I want?):

_____

Motivation (Why do I want it?):

_____

Action (How will I get it?):

_____

Goal #3

Goal (What do I want?):

_____

Motivation (Why do I want it?):

_____

Action (How will I get it?):

_____

Today's Date:_____

Scripture to Consider: _____

Reflections on Scripture:_____

_____

Adoration: _____

_____

_____

Confession:_____

_____

_____

Thanksgiving:_____

_____

_____

Supplication: _____

_____

_____

What's the most important thing I plan to do today?

_____

_____

Whom can I serve (encourage, bless, invest in, etc.) today?

_____

_____

How?

_____

_____

How am I doing on my weekly goals?

_____

_____

Notes:

_____

_____

_____

_____

_____

_____

_____

_____

_____

Today's Date:_____

Scripture to Consider:_____

Reflections on Scripture:_____

_____

Adoration:_____

_____

_____

Confession:_____

_____

_____

Thanksgiving:_____

_____

_____

Supplication:_____

_____

_____

What's the most important thing I plan to do today?

_____

_____

Whom can I serve (encourage, bless, invest in, etc.) today?

_____

_____

How?

_____

_____

How am I doing on my weekly goals?

_____

_____

Notes:

_____

_____

_____

_____

_____

_____

_____

_____

_____

_____

_____

Today's Date:_____

Scripture to Consider: _____

Reflections on Scripture:_____

_____

Adoration: _____

_____

_____

Confession: _____

_____

_____

Thanksgiving:_____

_____

_____

Supplication: _____

_____

_____

What's the most important thing I plan to do today?

_____

_____

Whom can I serve (encourage, bless, invest in, etc.) today?

_____

_____

How?

_____

_____

How am I doing on my weekly goals?

_____

_____

Notes:

_____

_____

_____

_____

_____

_____

_____

_____

_____

_____

Today's Date:_____

Scripture to Consider:_____

Reflections on Scripture:_____

_____

Adoration:_____

_____

_____

Confession:_____

_____

_____

Thanksgiving:_____

_____

_____

Supplication:_____

_____

_____

What's the most important thing I plan to do today?

_____

_____

Whom can I serve (encourage, bless, invest in, etc.) today?

_____

_____

How?

_____

_____

How am I doing on my weekly goals?

_____

_____

Notes:

_____

_____

_____

_____

_____

_____

_____

_____

_____

_____

Today's Date:_____

Scripture to Consider:_____

Reflections on Scripture:_____

_____

Adoration:_____

_____

_____

Confession:_____

_____

_____

Thanksgiving:_____

_____

_____

Supplication:_____

_____

_____

What's the most important thing I plan to do today?

_____

_____

Whom can I serve (encourage, bless, invest in, etc.) today?

_____

_____

How?

_____

_____

How am I doing on my weekly goals?

_____

_____

Notes:

_____

_____

_____

_____

_____

_____

_____

_____

_____

Today's Date: _____

Scripture to Consider: _____

Reflections on Scripture: _____

_____

Adoration: _____

_____

_____

Confession: _____

_____

_____

Thanksgiving: _____

_____

_____

Supplication: _____

_____

_____

What's the most important thing I plan to do today?

_____

_____

Whom can I serve (encourage, bless, invest in, etc.) today?

_____

_____

How?

_____

_____

How am I doing on my weekly goals?

_____

_____

Notes:

_____

_____

_____

_____

_____

_____

_____

_____

_____

_____

Today's Date:_____

Scripture to Consider:_____

Reflections on Scripture:_____

_____

Adoration:_____

_____

_____

Confession:_____

_____

_____

Thanksgiving:_____

_____

_____

Supplication:_____

_____

_____

What's the most important thing I plan to do today?

_____

_____

Whom can I serve (encourage, bless, invest in, etc.) today?

_____

_____

How?

_____

_____

How am I doing on my weekly goals?

_____

_____

Notes:

_____

_____

_____

_____

_____

_____

_____

_____

_____

_____

_____

What has God accomplished in my character in the last four weeks?

_____

_____

_____

How has God shown his faithfulness to me in the last four weeks?

_____

_____

_____

What passage of scripture has had the most impact over the last four weeks?

_____

_____

_____

What was my last powerful experience with God?

_____

_____

_____

What is increasing my affection toward God and others?

_____

_____

_____

What is decreasing my affection toward God and others?

_____

_____

_____

What is causing me fear or anxiety right now?

_____

_____

_____

Where is my heart hard or cold?

_____

_____

_____

What do I need most from God right now?

_____

_____

_____

Where am I most encouraged?

_____

_____

_____

Where am I most discouraged?

_____

_____

_____

What areas of my life most need to be transformed?

_____

_____

_____

What current obstacles hinder my spiritual growth?

_____

_____

_____

What competes with God for my affection and attention?

_____

_____

_____

What bad habits do I need to avoid?

_____

_____

_____

What good habits do I need to grow?

_____

_____

_____

Which relationships need to improve? How?

_____

_____

_____

What am I taking for granted?

_____

_____

_____

How am I doing with my quarterly goals?

_____

_____

_____

What actions do I need to take based on these questions?

_____

_____

_____

WEEK 9

Today's Date:_____

What am I praying for this week?

_____

_____

_____

What I am thankful for from last week?

_____

_____

_____

What am I excited about this week?

_____

_____

_____

What are my biggest challenges this week?

_____

_____

_____

How can I make the deepest impact this week?

_____

_____

_____

Top Three Goals This Week:

Goal #1

Goal (What do I want?):

_____

Motivation (Why do I want it?):

_____

Action (How will I get it?):

_____

Goal #2

Goal (What do I want?):

_____

Motivation (Why do I want it?):

_____

Action (How will I get it?):

_____

Goal #3

Goal (What do I want?):

_____

Motivation (Why do I want it?):

_____

Action (How will I get it?):

_____

Today's Date:_____

Scripture to Consider:_____

Reflections on Scripture:_____

_____

Adoration:_____

_____

_____

Confession:_____

_____

_____

Thanksgiving:_____

_____

_____

Supplication:_____

_____

_____

What's the most important thing I plan to do today?

_____

_____

Whom can I serve (encourage, bless, invest in, etc.) today?

_____

_____

How?

_____

_____

How am I doing on my weekly goals?

_____

_____

Notes:

_____

_____

_____

_____

_____

_____

_____

_____

_____

_____

WEEK 9
DAY 2

Today's Date:_____

Scripture to Consider:_____

Reflections on Scripture:_____

_____

Adoration:_____

_____

_____

Confession:_____

_____

_____

Thanksgiving:_____

_____

_____

Supplication:_____

_____

_____

What's the most important thing I plan to do today?

_____

_____

Whom can I serve (encourage, bless, invest in, etc.) today?

_____

_____

How?

_____

_____

How am I doing on my weekly goals?

_____

_____

Notes:

_____

_____

_____

_____

_____

_____

_____

_____

_____

_____

_____

WEEK 9
DAY 3

Today's Date:_____

Scripture to Consider:_____

Reflections on Scripture:_____

_____

Adoration:_____

_____

_____

Confession:_____

_____

_____

Thanksgiving:_____

_____

_____

Supplication:_____

_____

_____

What's the most important thing I plan to do today?

_____

_____

Whom can I serve (encourage, bless, invest in, etc.) today?

_____

_____

How?

_____

_____

How am I doing on my weekly goals?

_____

_____

Notes:

_____

_____

_____

_____

_____

_____

_____

_____

_____

_____

Today's Date:_____

Scripture to Consider:_____

Reflections on Scripture:_____

_____

Adoration:_____

_____

_____

Confession:_____

_____

_____

Thanksgiving:_____

_____

_____

Supplication:_____

_____

_____

What's the most important thing I plan to do today?

_____

_____

Whom can I serve (encourage, bless, invest in, etc.) today?

_____

_____

How?

_____

_____

How am I doing on my weekly goals?

_____

_____

Notes:

_____

_____

_____

_____

_____

_____

_____

_____

_____

_____

WEEK 9
DAY 5

Today's Date: _____

Scripture to Consider: _____

Reflections on Scripture: _____

_____

Adoration: _____

_____

_____

Confession: _____

_____

_____

Thanksgiving: _____

_____

_____

Supplication: _____

_____

_____

What's the most important thing I plan to do today?

_____

_____

Whom can I serve (encourage, bless, invest in, etc.) today?

_____

_____

How?

_____

_____

How am I doing on my weekly goals?

_____

_____

Notes:

_____

_____

_____

_____

_____

_____

_____

_____

_____

_____

WEEK 9
DAY 6

Today's Date:_____

Scripture to Consider:_____

Reflections on Scripture:_____
_____

Adoration:_____
_____
_____

Confession:_____
_____
_____

Thanksgiving:_____
_____
_____

Supplication:_____
_____
_____

What's the most important thing I plan to do today?

_____

_____

Whom can I serve (encourage, bless, invest in, etc.) today?

_____

_____

How?

_____

_____

How am I doing on my weekly goals?

_____

_____

Notes:

_____

_____

_____

_____

_____

_____

_____

_____

_____

_____

Today's Date:_____

Scripture to Consider:_____

Reflections on Scripture:_____

_____

Adoration:_____

_____

_____

Confession:_____

_____

_____

Thanksgiving:_____

_____

_____

Supplication:_____

_____

_____

What's the most important thing I plan to do today?

_____

_____

Whom can I serve (encourage, bless, invest in, etc.) today?

_____

_____

How?

_____

_____

How am I doing on my weekly goals?

_____

_____

Notes:

_____

_____

_____

_____

_____

_____

_____

_____

_____

_____

_____

WEEK 10

Today's Date:_____

What am I praying for this week?

_____

_____

_____

What I am thankful for from last week?

_____

_____

_____

What am I excited about this week?

_____

_____

_____

What are my biggest challenges this week?

_____

_____

_____

How can I make the deepest impact this week?

_____

_____

_____

Top Three Goals This Week:

Goal #1

Goal (What do I want?):

_____

Motivation (Why do I want it?):

_____

Action (How will I get it?):

_____

Goal #2

Goal (What do I want?):

_____

Motivation (Why do I want it?):

_____

Action (How will I get it?):

_____

Goal #3

Goal (What do I want?):

_____

Motivation (Why do I want it?):

_____

Action (How will I get it?):

_____

WEEK 10
DAY 1

Today's Date:_____

Scripture to Consider:_____

Reflections on Scripture:_____
_____

Adoration:_____
_____
_____

Confession:_____
_____
_____

Thanksgiving:_____
_____
_____

Supplication:_____
_____
_____

What's the most important thing I plan to do today?

_____

_____

Whom can I serve (encourage, bless, invest in, etc.) today?

_____

_____

How?

_____

_____

How am I doing on my weekly goals?

_____

_____

Notes:

_____

_____

_____

_____

_____

_____

_____

_____

_____

_____

_____

Today's Date:_____

Scripture to Consider: _____

Reflections on Scripture:_____

_____

Adoration: _____

_____

_____

Confession:_____

_____

_____

Thanksgiving:_____

_____

_____

Supplication:_____

_____

_____

What's the most important thing I plan to do today?

_____

_____

Whom can I serve (encourage, bless, invest in, etc.) today?

_____

_____

How?

_____

_____

How am I doing on my weekly goals?

_____

_____

Notes:

_____

_____

_____

_____

_____

_____

_____

_____

_____

_____

Today's Date:_____

Scripture to Consider: _____

Reflections on Scripture:_____

_____

Adoration:_____

_____

_____

Confession:_____

_____

_____

Thanksgiving:_____

_____

_____

Supplication:_____

_____

_____

What's the most important thing I plan to do today?

_____

_____

Whom can I serve (encourage, bless, invest in, etc.) today?

_____

_____

How?

_____

_____

How am I doing on my weekly goals?

_____

_____

Notes:

_____

_____

_____

_____

_____

_____

_____

_____

_____

_____

Today's Date:_____

Scripture to Consider: _____

Reflections on Scripture:_____
_____

Adoration:_____
_____
_____

Confession:_____
_____
_____

Thanksgiving:_____
_____
_____

Supplication:_____
_____
_____

What's the most important thing I plan to do today?

_____

_____

Whom can I serve (encourage, bless, invest in, etc.) today?

_____

_____

How?

_____

_____

How am I doing on my weekly goals?

_____

_____

Notes:

_____

_____

_____

_____

_____

_____

_____

_____

_____

_____

_____

Today's Date: _____

Scripture to Consider: _____

Reflections on Scripture: _____

_____

Adoration: _____

_____

_____

Confession: _____

_____

_____

Thanksgiving: _____

_____

_____

Supplication: _____

_____

_____

What's the most important thing I plan to do today?

_____

_____

Whom can I serve (encourage, bless, invest in, etc.) today?

_____

_____

How?

_____

_____

How am I doing on my weekly goals?

_____

_____

Notes:

_____

_____

_____

_____

_____

_____

_____

_____

_____

_____

WEEK 10
DAY 6

Today's Date:_____

Scripture to Consider:_____

Reflections on Scripture:_____

_____

Adoration:_____

_____

_____

Confession:_____

_____

_____

Thanksgiving:_____

_____

_____

Supplication:_____

_____

_____

What's the most important thing I plan to do today?

_____

_____

Whom can I serve (encourage, bless, invest in, etc.) today?

_____

_____

How?

_____

_____

How am I doing on my weekly goals?

_____

_____

Notes:

_____

_____

_____

_____

_____

_____

_____

_____

_____

_____

_____

Today's Date:_____

Scripture to Consider: _____

Reflections on Scripture:_____

_____

Adoration:_____

_____

_____

Confession:_____

_____

_____

Thanksgiving:_____

_____

_____

Supplication: _____

_____

_____

What's the most important thing I plan to do today?

_____

_____

Whom can I serve (encourage, bless, invest in, etc.) today?

_____

_____

How?

_____

_____

How am I doing on my weekly goals?

_____

_____

Notes:

_____

_____

_____

_____

_____

_____

_____

_____

_____

_____

WEEK 11

Today's Date:_____

What am I praying for this week?

_____

_____

_____

What I am thankful for from last week?

_____

_____

_____

What am I excited about this week?

_____

_____

_____

What are my biggest challenges this week?

_____

_____

_____

How can I make the deepest impact this week?

_____

_____

_____

Top Three Goals This Week:

Goal #1

Goal (What do I want?):

_____

Motivation (Why do I want it?):

_____

Action (How will I get it?):

_____

Goal #2

Goal (What do I want?):

_____

Motivation (Why do I want it?):

_____

Action (How will I get it?):

_____

Goal #3

Goal (What do I want?):

_____

Motivation (Why do I want it?):

_____

Action (How will I get it?):

_____

WEEK 11
DAY 1

Today's Date:_____

Scripture to Consider:_____

Reflections on Scripture:_____

_____

Adoration:_____

_____

_____

Confession:_____

_____

_____

Thanksgiving:_____

_____

_____

Supplication:_____

_____

_____

What's the most important thing I plan to do today?

_____

_____

Whom can I serve (encourage, bless, invest in, etc.) today?

_____

_____

How?

_____

_____

How am I doing on my weekly goals?

_____

_____

Notes:

_____

_____

_____

_____

_____

_____

_____

_____

_____

_____

WEEK 11
DAY 2

Today's Date:_____

Scripture to Consider: _____

Reflections on Scripture:_____

_____

Adoration:_____

_____

_____

Confession:_____

_____

_____

Thanksgiving:_____

_____

_____

Supplication:_____

_____

_____

What's the most important thing I plan to do today?

_____

_____

Whom can I serve (encourage, bless, invest in, etc.) today?

_____

_____

How?

_____

_____

How am I doing on my weekly goals?

_____

_____

Notes:

_____

_____

_____

_____

_____

_____

_____

_____

_____

_____

Today's Date:_____

Scripture to Consider: _____

Reflections on Scripture:_____

_____

Adoration: _____

_____

_____

Confession: _____

_____

_____

Thanksgiving:_____

_____

_____

Supplication: _____

_____

_____

What's the most important thing I plan to do today?

_____

_____

Whom can I serve (encourage, bless, invest in, etc.) today?

_____

_____

How?

_____

_____

How am I doing on my weekly goals?

_____

_____

Notes:

_____

_____

_____

_____

_____

_____

_____

_____

_____

_____

Today's Date:_____

Scripture to Consider:_____

Reflections on Scripture:_____

_____

Adoration:_____

_____

_____

Confession:_____

_____

_____

Thanksgiving:_____

_____

_____

Supplication:_____

_____

_____

What's the most important thing I plan to do today?

_____

_____

Whom can I serve (encourage, bless, invest in, etc.) today?

_____

_____

How?

_____

_____

How am I doing on my weekly goals?

_____

_____

Notes:

_____

_____

_____

_____

_____

_____

_____

_____

_____

_____

Today's Date:_____

Scripture to Consider: _____

Reflections on Scripture:_____

_____

Adoration:_____

_____

_____

Confession:_____

_____

_____

Thanksgiving:_____

_____

_____

Supplication:_____

_____

_____

What's the most important thing I plan to do today?

_____

_____

Whom can I serve (encourage, bless, invest in, etc.) today?

_____

_____

How?

_____

_____

How am I doing on my weekly goals?

_____

_____

Notes:

_____

_____

_____

_____

_____

_____

_____

_____

_____

_____

_____

Today's Date:_____

Scripture to Consider:_____

Reflections on Scripture:_____

_____

Adoration:_____

_____

_____

Confession:_____

_____

_____

Thanksgiving:_____

_____

_____

Supplication:_____

_____

_____

What's the most important thing I plan to do today?

_____

_____

Whom can I serve (encourage, bless, invest in, etc.) today?

_____

_____

How?

_____

_____

How am I doing on my weekly goals?

_____

_____

Notes:

_____

_____

_____

_____

_____

_____

_____

_____

_____

_____

Today's Date:_____

Scripture to Consider:_____

Reflections on Scripture:_____

_____

Adoration:_____

_____

_____

Confession:_____

_____

_____

Thanksgiving:_____

_____

_____

Supplication:_____

_____

_____

What's the most important thing I plan to do today?

_____

_____

Whom can I serve (encourage, bless, invest in, etc.) today?

_____

_____

How?

_____

_____

How am I doing on my weekly goals?

_____

_____

Notes:

_____

_____

_____

_____

_____

_____

_____

_____

_____

_____

WEEK 12

Today's Date: _____

What am I praying for this week?

_____

_____

_____

What I am thankful for from last week?

_____

_____

_____

What am I excited about this week?

_____

_____

_____

What are my biggest challenges this week?

_____

_____

_____

How can I make the deepest impact this week?

_____

_____

_____

Top Three Goals This Week:

Goal #1

Goal (What do I want?):

_____

Motivation (Why do I want it?):

_____

Action (How will I get it?):

_____

Goal #2

Goal (What do I want?):

_____

Motivation (Why do I want it?):

_____

Action (How will I get it?):

_____

Goal #3

Goal (What do I want?):

_____

Motivation (Why do I want it?):

_____

Action (How will I get it?):

_____

Today's Date:_____

Scripture to Consider:_____

Reflections on Scripture:_____

_____

Adoration:_____

_____

_____

Confession:_____

_____

_____

Thanksgiving:_____

_____

_____

Supplication:_____

_____

_____

What's the most important thing I plan to do today?

_____

_____

Whom can I serve (encourage, bless, invest in, etc.) today?

_____

_____

How?

_____

_____

How am I doing on my weekly goals?

_____

_____

Notes:

_____

_____

_____

_____

_____

_____

_____

_____

_____

_____

Today's Date:_____

Scripture to Consider:_____

Reflections on Scripture:_____

_____

Adoration:_____

_____

_____

Confession:_____

_____

_____

Thanksgiving:_____

_____

_____

Supplication:_____

_____

_____

What's the most important thing I plan to do today?

_____

_____

Whom can I serve (encourage, bless, invest in, etc.) today?

_____

_____

How?

_____

_____

How am I doing on my weekly goals?

_____

_____

Notes:

_____

_____

_____

_____

_____

_____

_____

_____

_____

_____

WEEK 12
DAY 3

Today's Date:_____

Scripture to Consider:_____

Reflections on Scripture:_____

_____

Adoration:_____

_____

_____

Confession:_____

_____

_____

Thanksgiving:_____

_____

_____

Supplication:_____

_____

_____

What's the most important thing I plan to do today?

_____

_____

Whom can I serve (encourage, bless, invest in, etc.) today?

_____

_____

How?

_____

_____

How am I doing on my weekly goals?

_____

_____

Notes:

_____

_____

_____

_____

_____

_____

_____

_____

_____

_____

Today's Date:_____

Scripture to Consider:_____

Reflections on Scripture:_____

_____

Adoration:_____

_____

_____

Confession:_____

_____

_____

Thanksgiving:_____

_____

_____

Supplication:_____

_____

_____

What's the most important thing I plan to do today?

_____

_____

Whom can I serve (encourage, bless, invest in, etc.) today?

_____

_____

How?

_____

_____

How am I doing on my weekly goals?

_____

_____

Notes:

_____

_____

_____

_____

_____

_____

_____

_____

_____

_____

Today's Date:_____

Scripture to Consider: _____

Reflections on Scripture:_____

_____

Adoration:_____

_____

_____

Confession:_____

_____

_____

Thanksgiving:_____

_____

_____

Supplication:_____

_____

_____

What's the most important thing I plan to do today?

_____

_____

Whom can I serve (encourage, bless, invest in, etc.) today?

_____

_____

How?

_____

_____

How am I doing on my weekly goals?

_____

_____

Notes:

_____

_____

_____

_____

_____

_____

_____

_____

_____

_____

Today's Date:_____

Scripture to Consider:_____

Reflections on Scripture:_____

_____

Adoration:_____

_____

_____

Confession:_____

_____

_____

Thanksgiving:_____

_____

_____

Supplication:_____

_____

_____

What's the most important thing I plan to do today?

_____

_____

Whom can I serve (encourage, bless, invest in, etc.) today?

_____

_____

How?

_____

_____

How am I doing on my weekly goals?

_____

_____

Notes:

_____

_____

_____

_____

_____

_____

_____

_____

_____

_____

Today's Date:_____

Scripture to Consider:_____

Reflections on Scripture:_____

_____

Adoration:_____

_____

_____

Confession:_____

_____

_____

Thanksgiving:_____

_____

_____

Supplication:_____

_____

_____

What's the most important thing I plan to do today?

_____

_____

Whom can I serve (encourage, bless, invest in, etc.) today?

_____

_____

How?

_____

_____

How am I doing on my weekly goals?

_____

_____

Notes:

_____

_____

_____

_____

_____

_____

_____

_____

_____

_____

_____

WEEK 13

Today's Date: _____

What am I praying for this week?

_____

_____

_____

What I am thankful for from last week?

_____

_____

_____

What am I excited about this week?

_____

_____

_____

What are my biggest challenges this week?

_____

_____

_____

How can I make the deepest impact this week?

_____

_____

_____

Top Three Goals This Week:

Goal #1

Goal (What do I want?):

_____

Motivation (Why do I want it?):

_____

Action (How will I get it?):

_____

Goal #2

Goal (What do I want?):

_____

Motivation (Why do I want it?):

_____

Action (How will I get it?):

_____

Goal #3

Goal (What do I want?):

_____

Motivation (Why do I want it?):

_____

Action (How will I get it?):

_____

Today's Date:_____

Scripture to Consider: _____

Reflections on Scripture:_____

_____

Adoration:_____

_____

_____

Confession: _____

_____

_____

Thanksgiving:_____

_____

_____

Supplication: _____

_____

_____

What's the most important thing I plan to do today?

_____

_____

Whom can I serve (encourage, bless, invest in, etc.) today?

_____

_____

How?

_____

_____

How am I doing on my weekly goals?

_____

_____

Notes:

_____

_____

_____

_____

_____

_____

_____

_____

_____

_____

Today's Date:_____

Scripture to Consider:_____

Reflections on Scripture:_____

_____

Adoration:_____

_____

_____

Confession:_____

_____

_____

Thanksgiving:_____

_____

_____

Supplication:_____

_____

_____

What's the most important thing I plan to do today?

_____

_____

Whom can I serve (encourage, bless, invest in, etc.) today?

_____

_____

How?

_____

_____

How am I doing on my weekly goals?

_____

_____

Notes:

_____

_____

_____

_____

_____

_____

_____

_____

_____

_____

WEEK 13
DAY 3

Today's Date:_____

Scripture to Consider: _____

Reflections on Scripture:_____

_____

Adoration:_____

_____

_____

Confession:_____

_____

_____

Thanksgiving:_____

_____

_____

Supplication: _____

_____

_____

What's the most important thing I plan to do today?

_____

_____

Whom can I serve (encourage, bless, invest in, etc.) today?

_____

_____

How?

_____

_____

How am I doing on my weekly goals?

_____

_____

Notes:

_____

_____

_____

_____

_____

_____

_____

_____

_____

_____

_____

Today's Date:_____

Scripture to Consider: _____

Reflections on Scripture:_____

_____

Adoration:_____

_____

_____

Confession:_____

_____

_____

Thanksgiving:_____

_____

_____

Supplication: _____

_____

_____

What's the most important thing I plan to do today?

_____

_____

Whom can I serve (encourage, bless, invest in, etc.) today?

_____

_____

How?

_____

_____

How am I doing on my weekly goals?

_____

_____

Notes:

_____

_____

_____

_____

_____

_____

_____

_____

_____

_____

WEEK 13
DAY 5

Today's Date: _____

Scripture to Consider: _____

Reflections on Scripture: _____
_____

Adoration: _____
_____
_____

Confession: _____
_____
_____

Thanksgiving: _____
_____
_____

Supplication: _____
_____
_____

What's the most important thing I plan to do today?

_____

_____

Whom can I serve (encourage, bless, invest in, etc.) today?

_____

_____

How?

_____

_____

How am I doing on my weekly goals?

_____

_____

Notes:

_____

_____

_____

_____

_____

_____

_____

_____

_____

_____

Today's Date:_____

Scripture to Consider: _____

Reflections on Scripture:_____

_____

Adoration: _____

_____

_____

Confession:_____

_____

_____

Thanksgiving:_____

_____

_____

Supplication: _____

_____

_____

What's the most important thing I plan to do today?

_____

_____

Whom can I serve (encourage, bless, invest in, etc.) today?

_____

_____

How?

_____

_____

How am I doing on my weekly goals?

_____

_____

Notes:

_____

_____

_____

_____

_____

_____

_____

_____

_____

_____

Today's Date:_____

Scripture to Consider: _____

Reflections on Scripture:_____

_____

Adoration: _____

_____

_____

Confession: _____

_____

_____

Thanksgiving:_____

_____

_____

Supplication:_____

_____

_____

What's the most important thing I plan to do today?

_____

_____

Whom can I serve (encourage, bless, invest in, etc.) today?

_____

_____

How?

_____

_____

How am I doing on my weekly goals?

_____

_____

Notes:

_____

_____

_____

_____

_____

_____

_____

_____

_____

_____

20 MONTHLY QUESTIONS
FOR SELF-REFLECTION

What has God accomplished in my character in the last four weeks?

_____

_____

_____

How has God shown his faithfulness to me in the last four weeks?

_____

_____

_____

What passage of scripture has had the most impact over the last four weeks?

_____

_____

_____

What was my last powerful experience with God?

_____

_____

_____

What is increasing my affection toward God and others?

_____

_____

_____

What is decreasing my affection toward God and others?

_____

_____

_____

What is causing me fear or anxiety right now?

_____

_____

_____

Where is my heart hard or cold?

_____

_____

_____

What do I need most from God right now?

_____

_____

_____

Where am I most encouraged?

_____

_____

_____

Where am I most discouraged?

_____

_____

_____

What areas of my life most need to be transformed?

_____

_____

_____

What current obstacles hinder my spiritual growth?

_____

_____

_____

What competes with God for my affection and attention?

_____

_____

_____

What bad habits do I need to avoid?

_____

_____

_____

What good habits do I need to grow?

_____

_____

_____

Which relationships need to improve? How?

_____

_____

_____

What am I taking for granted?

_____

_____

_____

How am I doing with my quarterly goals?

_____

_____

_____

What actions do I need to take based on these questions?

_____

_____

_____